Inspired Ventures

Startups that Began as A Dream

Author – Stan Barren

Brought to you by InspirationDB

Stan Barren

Legal and Copyright Disclaimer

Stan Barren

Exclusive Offer Inside!

Have you ever found yourself questioning the direction of your life or wondering if there's more to your journey? We have something special just for you - a roadmap to finding that missing piece, a guide to uncovering the purpose that fuels your passion and drives your ambitions.

Introducing "The Ultimate Guide to Finding Your Life's Purpose."

Whether you're at a crossroads, feeling lost, or simply curious about what makes life truly meaningful, this comprehensive e-book has the insights, exercises, and stories to illuminate your path.

And here's the best part: We're giving it away for FREE! Don't miss out! Subscribe to our email newsletter now and get instant access to "The Ultimate Guide to Finding Your Life's Purpose." Discover the passion, meaning, and drive that's waiting within you.

Get it now by visiting InspirationDB.com/FREE

Stan Barren

Table of Contents

Introduction

In the vast tapestry of human history, few narratives captivate us quite like the tales of audacious dreamers who challenge the status quo to birth innovative enterprises.

These are stories of unyielding individuals who, starting with a mere spark of an idea, fan it with passion and resilience until it ignites into a blazing reality. "Inspired Ventures: Startups that Began as a Dream" seeks to delve into these stirring journeys, presenting a mosaic of tales from the gritty alleyways of entrepreneurship.

Every chapter in this book is an homage to the spirit of innovation and the undying will to bring dreams to fruition. Within these pages, you won't just find success stories, but narratives replete with failures, pivots, moments of doubt, and triumphant comebacks.

While every startup's journey is as unique as a fingerprint, certain underlying themes resonate across all: the importance of vision, the hurdles of creation, the joy of success, and the invaluable lessons from setbacks.

As we venture together into this exploration, you'll be introduced to a diverse array of ventures from around the globe. From the bustling tech hubs of Silicon Valley to the vibrant markets of Africa, these are tales of businesses that began as mere ideas, often scribbled on napkins, discussed over coffee, or dreamed up in basements.

We hope that by the end of this odyssey, you'll not only be inspired by these tales but also gain insights and wisdom to fuel your own entrepreneurial journey. Welcome to the world of "Inspired Ventures."

The Universal Allure of Startups: Why We Are Drawn to Stories of Humble Beginnings

The universal allure of startups is an intriguing phenomenon, intertwining dreams of unparalleled success with stories of humble beginnings, allowing us to witness the metamorphosis of a simple idea into a world-changing venture.

These stories beckon to us with the charm of possibility, the promise of transformative impact, and the allure of overcoming insurmountable challenges.

Startups represent more than just business entities; they symbolize the quintessential human spirit of relentless pursuit and unyielding resilience.

Their beginnings, often wrapped in struggles and uncertainties, resonate deeply with our inherent desire to root for the underdog, to see perseverance conquer adversity.

There's an innate appeal in observing a raw concept, born out of necessity or sheer curiosity, navigate through the turbulent waters of skepticism, financial constraints, and operational challenges, eventually emerging as a beacon of innovation and change.

The narrative of humble beginnings fosters a sense of relatability and attainability. It renders the audacious journey of entrepreneurship accessible, allowing us to see fragments of our aspirations and ideas mirrored in the odysseys of those who dared to venture into the unknown.

These stories act as conduits for our latent desires, igniting the spark of potentiality, making us believe in the boundlessness of what we can achieve.

Moreover, the allure is intensified by the transformative impact these startups wield, not just on markets but on lives and societies, reshaping norms and redefining boundaries.

They embody the nexus of imagination and pragmatism, inspiring a generation of dreamers and doers to traverse beyond the conventional, to reimagine the contours of what's possible.

In essence, our fascination with startups and their often-modest origins is a reflection of our collective longing for inspiration and our inherent belief in the transformative power of human endeavor.

It's this universal resonance of hope, aspiration, and transformation that makes the stories of startups not just appealing, but fundamentally human.

Objective Of "Inspired Ventures: Startups That Began as A Dream"

In the digital age, there's a relentless cascade of information, advice, and lore surrounding entrepreneurship. Yet, amidst the buzzwords and trend reports, the real essence of starting a business, the raw passion, resilience, and vision, often gets overshadowed.

The primary objective of "Inspired Ventures: Startups that Began as a Dream" is to delve into this very essence, pulling back the curtain on the authentic journeys of entrepreneurs who dared to bring their visions to life.

The act of starting a business is more than just finding a gap in the market; it's about solving problems, meeting deep-seated human needs, and sometimes, even changing the world a little bit at a time. These are not merely ventures built on market analysis and profit forecasts, but on dreams.

By offering readers a front-row seat to these captivating tales, the book seeks to inspire the next generation of dreamers.

Whether they are hesitant first-time entrepreneurs, seasoned business people in need of rekindling their passion, or mere enthusiasts, the narratives within these pages will ignite a spark, affirming the belief that dreams, when pursued with fervor, can indeed shape realities.

Furthermore, while inspiration is a driving force behind the book, education remains a crucial pillar. Real-world entrepreneurship is rife with pitfalls, mistakes, and learning curves.

By traversing the landscapes of various startups, readers will glean practical insights, strategies, and lessons that textbooks often overlook.

The intertwining of anecdotal wisdom with actionable advice is designed to equip aspiring entrepreneurs, guiding them as they embark on their own ventures.

In essence, "Inspired Ventures" is more than a compilation of success stories. It's a tribute to the indomitable spirit of entrepreneurship, a guidebook dotted with milestones of innovation, and most importantly, a beacon for all who dare to dream.

Brief Overview of The Startups to Be Covered

In this book, we will embark on a journey through the inception stories of some of the most transformative startups of the digital age. These companies began as mere ideas, dreams that were nurtured into reality by their tenacious founders.

Each of these startups, Dropbox, Airbnb, Slack, MailChimp, WhatsApp, Spotify, and SocialNet, has a unique narrative that exemplifies innovation, resilience, and the indomitable spirit of entrepreneurship.

Dropbox started with a forgotten USB drive and a personal pain point. Drew Houston's simple wish to access his files from anywhere led to the creation of one of the world's leading cloud storage services, a service that allows millions of users to effortlessly store, share, and sync their digital lives.

Airbnb turned the concept of home-sharing from a risky proposition to a global phenomenon. The founders, Brian Chesky, Joe Gebbia, and Nathan Blecharczyk, transformed the way people travel, turning every home into a potential hotel and providing travelers with unique, local experiences that go beyond the generic hotel room.

Slack reimagined workplace communication, elevating it from disjointed emails to streamlined, channel-based messaging. Stewart Butterfield and his team took an internal tool built for a completely different purpose and spun it into a platform that has revolutionized team collaboration.

MailChimp began as a side project for a web design agency and grew into an email marketing behemoth.

Founders Ben Chestnut and Dan Kurzius showed that understanding your customers and evolving with their needs can turn even the humblest of tools into an indispensable service for businesses worldwide.

WhatsApp's story is one of simplicity and focus. Jan Koum and Brian Acton, both veterans of Yahoo, saw the potential in a frills-free, reliable messaging app at a time when the market was cluttered with complicated, unstable options.

Their commitment to user privacy and straightforward design made WhatsApp a household name in global communication.

Spotify revolutionized the music industry by wrestling it away from the grips of piracy and transforming it into a service that benefits artists and listeners alike. Daniel Ek and Martin Lorentzon created a platform that gave users access to a world of music while ensuring that artists got their fair share.

SocialNet, though lesser-known and ultimately overshadowed by later ventures like LinkedIn, laid important groundwork in the social networking space.

Founded by Reid Hoffman, it was an early harbinger of how online platforms could connect people professionally and personally, sowing the seeds for the social media revolution.

Each of these companies had a modest beginning, a fundamental challenge to overcome, and a society-shaping vision. They didn't just create products; they created new behaviors, habits, and economies.

Their paths to success were fraught with challenges, from funding woes to user adoption struggles, but their founders persevered, guided by the north star of their initial inspiration.

As we delve into each story, we'll uncover not just the strategic decisions that paved their way to success but also the emotional and intellectual fortitude that drove their founders to keep dreaming, even when the odds were stacked against them.

These are not just stories of business; they are narratives of personal triumph, collective resilience, and the human capacity to envision a different future.

Chapter 1: The Age of Startups

In the annals of business history, there have been epochs defined by titanic industrialists, transformative inventions, and global events that have reshaped economies. But as we stand in the 21st century, a new epoch is unfolding before our very eyes - the Age of Startups.

While the term 'startup' may evoke images of tech-savvy youngsters working in garages and coffeehouses, it embodies much more than that. At its core, a startup is the embodiment of a dream, a singular vision striving to solve a tangible problem or fill a specific need in the marketplace.

Yet, what makes this age particularly distinct? Why are we seeing such an exponential surge in startups now? Several interwoven factors contribute to this phenomenon, from the ubiquity of the internet, democratizing access to information, to evolving socio-cultural norms that value innovation over tenure.

The reduced barriers to business entry, the digital revolution, and the rising gig economy have created a fertile ground for entrepreneurial aspirations to thrive.

In this chapter, we will traverse the timeline of entrepreneurship, drawing parallels with past eras, and delve deep into the forces catalyzing the present-day startup boom. As we explore the dynamics of this age, we will uncover the challenges, triumphs, and the indomitable spirit that characterizes the world of startups.

Prepare to embark on a journey through time, understanding how today's entrepreneurial landscape has been shaped and what it signifies for the future of business and innovation.

Stan Barren

The Evolution of Entrepreneurship: A Historical Context

The roots of entrepreneurship are ancient, stretching back to the times of trade and barter, where individuals organized and operated ventures to exploit opportunities for trade. The very essence of entrepreneurship has been the recognition of opportunity and the willingness to harness resources to pursue it.

This fundamental notion has travelled through epochs, molding itself according to the socio-economic fabric of the respective times.

In the early stages of industrialization during the 17th and 18th centuries, entrepreneurship experienced a significant transformation. The era marked a shift from small-scale tradesmen to industrial magnates, with innovations in manufacturing, transportation, and communication fostering a newfound spirit of enterprise.

This period saw the emergence of iconic entrepreneurs like James Watt and Richard Arkwright, whose ventures laid the groundwork for large-scale industries and demonstrated the profound societal impact entrepreneurship could yield.

The 20th century ushered in another pivotal phase in the evolution of entrepreneurship, with the rise of the digital era and the advent of the Internet reshaping commercial landscapes.

The late 1900s and early 2000s were characterized by the Dotcom boom and subsequent bust, which were emblematic of the high-risk, high-reward nature of entrepreneurial ventures.

The period witnessed the inception of tech behemoths like Amazon and eBay, illustrating the transformative potential of technology-oriented startups.

Throughout these varying phases, the essence of entrepreneurship has remained constant, the pursuit of innovation and the creation of value. However, the modalities, the scopes, and the spheres have seen relentless evolution.

The current epoch is characterized by a renewed entrepreneurial spirit, where sustainability, social responsibility, and inclusivity are at the forefront. Startups today are not just pursuing financial success; they are aspiring to contribute to societal well-being and environmental conservation, aligning profit with purpose.

The historical context of entrepreneurship reveals a rich tapestry of change, resilience, and innovation. The journey from the local tradesman of ancient civilizations to the tech innovators of the 21st century marks the undying human spirit to conceive, create, and contribute, transcending temporal and spatial boundaries.

The evolution of entrepreneurship is, in essence, a reflection of humanity's ceaseless endeavor to shape its destiny, reflect its values, and realize its visions in the ongoing pursuit of progress.

The Rise of the Digital Era and Its Impact on Startups

The dawn of the digital era, marked by the rapid proliferation of the internet and the widespread adoption of digital technologies, has heralded a transformative epoch in the realm of entrepreneurship.

As the boundaries of the physical world began to blur, a new digital landscape emerged, offering infinite realms of possibilities and opportunities. The digital era hasn't just offered a new platform but has revolutionized the very fundamentals of how businesses operate, interact, and evolve.

Startups, often characterized by their agility and adaptability, were among the first to harness the potential of this digital shift. Gone were the days where substantial capital was a prerequisite to launch a business.

With a computer, an innovative idea, and a dash of daring, entrepreneurs could now set up digital storefronts, offer services globally, or even pioneer entirely new industries, all from the comfort of their homes. The barriers to entry drastically lowered, democratizing entrepreneurship and making it accessible to many more individuals than ever before.

Moreover, the digital era engendered a paradigm shift in consumer behavior and expectations. With the world's information and a plethora of services at their fingertips, consumers began to prioritize convenience, personalization, and immediacy.

Recognizing these evolving demands, startups leveraged data analytics, artificial intelligence, and other emerging technologies to offer hyper-targeted solutions, often outpacing established businesses in innovation.

Furthermore, the very nature of business growth transformed. Virality, a concept once reserved for contagious diseases or the occasional pop culture phenomenon, became a coveted metric in the digital startup world, with companies vying to create the next trending app or viral service.

But it wasn't just about the ease of starting up or reaching consumers. The digital age brought about a seismic shift in funding mechanisms as well. Crowdfunding platforms like Kickstarter or Indiegogo allowed entrepreneurs to validate and fund ideas directly through potential consumers.

Traditional gatekeepers of capital, like banks, were supplemented, if not sometimes bypassed, by venture capitalists eager to invest in the next big digital innovation.

In essence, the rise of the digital era has not only expanded the horizons for startups but has fundamentally reshaped the entrepreneurial landscape. With each passing algorithm update, tech innovation, or digital trend, startups continue to be at the forefront, navigating and molding the digital frontier.

Key Factors Enabling Today's Entrepreneurial Ecosystem

The entrepreneurial landscape of today is drastically different from what it was even just a couple of decades ago. Several critical factors have converged, creating a fertile ground for budding entrepreneurs to bring their ideas to life.

First and foremost is the technological revolution. The unprecedented rise of the internet, cloud computing, and mobile technology has not only democratized information access but has also drastically reduced the initial costs to launch startups.

It's now possible to start a global business right from one's living room. Furthermore, technologies like 3D printing, AI, and blockchain are opening up entirely new industries ripe for disruption.

The second factor is the accessibility to funding. Gone are the days when only a few had accesses to venture capitalists in Silicon Valley or Wall Street. Now, with platforms like Kickstarter, Indiegogo, and GoFundMe, crowdfunding has democratized startup funding.

Moreover, the global rise of angel investors and venture capital firms means that good ideas have a better chance than ever to secure the necessary financial backing.

The emergence of startup incubators and accelerators, from Y Combinator to TechStars, further offer not just funding but also mentorship and networking opportunities.

Educational resources and platforms form the third pillar. The last decade has witnessed an explosion in online courses, workshops, and webinars aimed at equipping entrepreneurs with the skills they need.

Platforms like Coursera, Udemy, and edX offer courses on everything from growth hacking to financial management. This educational democratization has flattened the learning curve significantly.

Finally, the global shift in mindset towards entrepreneurship cannot be understated. The modern culture celebrates entrepreneurial risk-taking.

Failures, once stigmatized, are now viewed as essential steps in the learning process. Entrepreneurs like Elon Musk, Steve Jobs, and Mark Zuckerberg have become household names, inspiring countless others to follow in their footsteps.

In essence, the interplay of technology, funding accessibility, education, and a supportive culture has created an environment where today's entrepreneurs can dare to dream bigger than ever before.

Stan Barren

Chapter 2: The Anatomy of a Startup Dream

What fuels the indomitable spirit of an entrepreneur? How does a mere thought evolve into a compelling vision, and eventually, into a tangible, thriving enterprise?

The seeds of every great startup lie in the intangible world of dreams, aspirations, and an unquenchable thirst to create.

In this chapter, we delve into the intricate anatomy of a startup dream, dissecting the layers that give it life and form.

At the heart of every startup is a compelling narrative, a story of seeing the world not just for what it is but for what it could be. Whether it stems from a personal pain point, a glaring gap in the market, or simply a novel perspective, this initial spark is crucial.

It's the ember that, when fanned with passion and tenacity, grows into the blazing fire that drives the startup journey.

However, while the romantic notion of a 'eureka' moment is appealing, the reality is often far more nuanced. The formulation of a startup idea is a confluence of experiences, insights, and often, a touch of serendipity.

In this chapter, we will explore the psychological underpinnings of these formative moments and decipher the ingredients that transform a fleeting thought into a groundbreaking venture.

Through intimate stories of founders and the birth of their brainchildren, we will journey into the heart of what truly constitutes the anatomy of a startup dream.

Prepare to be inspired, to resonate with familiar emotions, and to understand the profound depth and breadth of the dreams that have shaped some of the most impactful startups of our age.

Psychological Underpinnings: What Ignites the Spark?

At the heart of every startup lies a singular moment, a spark of inspiration. This spark, however, doesn't materialize out of thin air.

Its origins can be traced back to intricate psychological underpinnings that push an individual to see beyond the ordinary, challenge the status quo, and venture into the world of entrepreneurship.

While each entrepreneurial journey is unique, many are built upon common psychological foundations.

Curiosity, for one, plays a pivotal role. An entrepreneur's mind is perpetually inquisitive, always probing, questioning, and seeking answers to problems both big and small.

It's this innate curiosity that often leads them to spot gaps in the market, inefficiencies in systems, or novel uses for everyday items. Where most people might see a problem as a mere inconvenience, an entrepreneur sees an opportunity, a chance to innovate and provide a solution.

Another significant driver is the need for autonomy. Many entrepreneurs are driven by the desire to be their own boss, to make decisions without constraints, and to shape their destiny. This yearning for independence pushes them to carve out their own path rather than follow a pre-defined one.

Risk tolerance also sets entrepreneurs apart. While the uncertainty of a new venture might deter many, those with an entrepreneurial spirit view risk differently.

They see it not as a deterrent but as a challenge, something to be managed and, if possible, turned to their advantage.

Their optimism, combined with a healthy acceptance of failure as a learning opportunity, often propels them forward even in the face of adversity.

Lastly, there's a deep-seated need for impact. Entrepreneurs are often driven by the desire to make a difference, to leave a mark on the world, and to create something bigger than themselves.

Whether it's bringing a new product to market, revolutionizing an industry, or simply making life a little easier or more enjoyable for people, there's a profound sense of purpose and fulfillment in knowing that their venture has the potential to change lives.

In essence, while the spark for each startup might be ignited by a different idea or opportunity, the psychological fuel that feeds the entrepreneurial fire is a complex blend of curiosity, autonomy, risk tolerance, and a desire for impact.

Key Ingredients for Startups: Passion, Problem, Solution, and Vision

Passion is the engine that drives an entrepreneur's will, especially during the tumultuous times of a startup journey. It's more than mere enthusiasm; it's a profound and unwavering commitment to a cause or idea.

Passion fuels long hours, provides resilience in the face of rejection, and inspires a founder to persist when others might give up.

For an entrepreneur, passion isn't just about loving what they do, it's about being so invested that the line between work and personal life often blurs, all in pursuit of a larger goal.

At the core of most successful startups lies a clearly identified Problem. The most transformative businesses emerge from genuine issues experienced first-hand by the founders or observed in the market.

Recognizing a problem is the first step, but understanding its depth, nuances, and implications is what differentiates a fleeting idea from a viable business opportunity.

For startups, this isn't just about spotting gaps, it's about empathizing with those affected by the problem and understanding the pain points in detail.

The Solution is where innovation shines. It's the tangible answer to the identified problem, uniquely tailored by the startup. Crafting a solution requires creativity, technical skill, and iterative testing.

It's not always about reinventing the wheel, sometimes, the most effective solutions are those that simply improve upon existing frameworks, making them more efficient, accessible, or user-friendly.

For a startup, the solution isn't static; it evolves based on feedback, market dynamics, and technological advancements.

Lastly, Vision is the north star for any startup. While the problem addresses the present and the solution deals with the immediate future, vision is the long-term roadmap.

It's the broader ambition, the world the founders envisage once their solution is widely adopted. Vision is what rallies a team together, attracts investors, and resonates with early adopters.

In a startup's journey, the path might change, but the vision remains a constant beacon, guiding strategies and decisions towards a larger purpose.

Together, these ingredients form the foundational pillars for startups. While each component is crucial, their true power is realized when they synergize, turning mere ideas into transformative ventures.

Case Study: Dropbox –Simple Observation and A Personal Pain Point

In the mid-2000s, Drew Houston, a student at the Massachusetts Institute of Technology (MIT), found himself repeatedly facing a frustrating issue: he kept forgetting his USB flash drive.

In the era before cloud storage became ubiquitous, forgetting a flash drive meant losing access to crucial files. Houston, like many others, was irked by the inconvenience of not having his files when and where he needed them. This personal frustration turned into a realization that others were likely facing the same challenge.

In a bus journey between Boston and New York, Houston began writing the initial lines of code that would eventually evolve into Dropbox.

The idea was straightforward yet powerful - a tool that would seamlessly synchronize files across different devices through the cloud, ensuring that users had access to their data wherever they went.

Houston envisioned Dropbox as an effortless solution to the cumbersome processes of emailing files to oneself or relying on physical storage devices.

The potential of Dropbox was immediately evident when Houston shared his prototype with fellow students and on online forums. The pain point he had identified was indeed universal, and his solution garnered substantial interest.

It wasn't long before he was invited to the prestigious Y Combinator startup accelerator program, where he met Arash Ferdowsi, who would become his co-founder.

Dropbox's journey from a simple observation on a bus to becoming a multi-billion-dollar company exemplifies how personal frustrations can translate into universally appreciated solutions.

By understanding and experiencing the problem first-hand, Houston was able to create a product that resonated with millions, truly emphasizing that sometimes, the best ideas come from solving one's own problems.

Chapter 3: From Idea to Reality

In every entrepreneur's journey, the phase of transmuting a conceptualized idea into a tangible reality represents a complex tapestry of trials, revelations, and pivotal decisions.

The birthing process of a startup is invariably steeped in a mix of exhilarating highs and formidable lows, marked by a relentless pursuit of vision and frequent encounters with doubt.

This chapter delves deep into the metamorphic journey of startups, offering readers a lens into the myriad challenges, triumphs, and moments of serendipity that characterize the formative phase of entrepreneurial ventures.

The realm of startups is synonymous with uncertainty and dynamism, each journey uniquely sculpted by the individual visions and the contexts within which they are nested. It is in this terrain of endless possibilities that ideas, raw and untamed, seek to transcend the confines of the abstract, striving to manifest into entities that influence, disrupt, and contribute.

In this pursuit, entrepreneurs find themselves navigating a labyrinth of financial constraints, operational intricacies, and psychological battles, often teetering on the edge between inspiration and disillusionment.

The essence of this chapter is to illuminate the untold stories and uncharted territories of the startup voyage, focusing on the intricate transition from the conceptual realm to the concrete world.

By examining real-life narratives and lived experiences of various entrepreneurs, we endeavor to extract invaluable lessons and insights about resilience, adaptability, and innovation.

We will witness the relentless spirit of founders, their unwavering faith in their dreams, and their resilience in facing and overcoming the inevitable obstacles and rejections that pave the road to realization.

In this exploration, we will unravel the diverse pathways traversed by different startups, shedding light on the importance of strategic planning, the value of relentless execution, and the significance of learning and iterating.

We will dissect the pivotal moments that define the trajectory of startups, providing aspiring entrepreneurs with a compendium of experiences that reflect the multifaceted nature of building a startup from scratch. The narratives encapsulated in this chapter serve as a beacon, guiding and inspiring those who dare to embark on the tumultuous yet rewarding odyssey from idea to reality.

Through the tapestry of stories and reflections presented in this chapter, readers will gain a nuanced understanding of the symbiotic relationship between failure and success, the transformative power of a well-nurtured idea, and the enduring impact of unwavering perseverance and belief.

It is a tribute to the dreamers who dare to defy the odds, the innovators who reshape landscapes, and the visionaries who breathe life into ideas, forever altering the way we perceive and interact with the world.

Let us embark on this exploration of transformation and discover the myriad ways in which the seeds of an idea blossom into entities that transcend their initial imaginations, shaping realms and leaving indelible marks on the sands of time.

The Journey from Concept to Concrete Business

The metamorphosis of a mere idea into a thriving business is one of the most exhilarating adventures an entrepreneur can undertake. It often begins in the realm of abstract thought, a fleeting notion, a sudden insight, or perhaps a personal frustration.

This nascent idea, though intangible, carries within it the potential to disrupt markets, change consumer behavior, and redefine industries. However, the path from ideation to realization is rarely linear, and it is peppered with trials, learning, and endless iteration.

The first steps involve molding the nebulous concept into a more definite form. This can entail creating a business model, identifying a target market, and understanding the problem the concept aims to solve.

Critical questions arise: Is there a genuine need for this product or service? What sets it apart from existing solutions? How will it deliver value to its users? Answering these queries requires thorough market research, competitor analysis, and often, direct feedback from potential customers.

Once the foundational strategy is in place, the entrepreneur confronts the challenge of actualization. This means transforming sketches into prototypes, concepts into MVPs (Minimum Viable Products), and visions into operational plans.

Here, funding often becomes a pivotal concern. Most ventures, no matter how modest, require some capital to move from the drawing board to the marketplace. Whether bootstrapped or financed by investors, judicious use of resources becomes paramount.

But perhaps the most intangible yet vital component of this journey is the resilience and adaptability of the entrepreneur. The transition from concept to concrete business is riddled with unanticipated hurdles, feedback loops, and pivots.

It's a dynamic dance of holding steadfast to one's vision while being open to change, learning from failures, and continuously evolving to meet market demands. In essence, the journey is less about the destination and more about the growth, insights, and experiences amassed along the way.

Challenges Faced in the Early Days: Financial, Operational, and Psychological

In the fledgling days of a startup, founders confront a trifecta of challenges that test their mettle and determination. These challenges, often intertwined, can be categorized as financial, operational, and psychological.

Financial Challenges: At the heart of many early-stage startup woes lies the formidable financial challenge. Seed capital, often sourced from personal savings, friends, or family, quickly dwindles as expenses mount. There's the rent for office space, salaries for the initial team, costs for product development, and marketing expenses, among others.

The quest for additional funding can be daunting. Venture capitalists and angel investors demand proof of concept, a viable business model, and often, significant traction before they invest. This creates a catch-22 situation where the startup needs funds to make progress but requires progress to secure funds.

Operational Challenges: The operational hurdles in a startup's infancy are no less daunting. Building a product or service that fits the market need, known as achieving product-market fit, is a journey riddled with trial and error.

Early-stage startups frequently lack the expertise in-house for all the functions they need, from marketing to tech development. Hiring the right talent can be both challenging and expensive.

Additionally, setting up efficient processes, managing resources, and navigating the regulatory landscape can be overwhelming for founders who are often wearing multiple hats.

Psychological Challenges: Perhaps the most underestimated yet profound challenges are psychological. The pressure to succeed, especially when personal funds are invested, can be immense.

Founders often grapple with imposter syndrome, questioning their worthiness to lead a company. The roller-coaster ride of highs and lows, with product failures, rejection from investors, or co-founder conflicts, can lead to stress, anxiety, and burnout.

The loneliness of entrepreneurship, where decisions rest on the founder's shoulders, can be isolating, making mental well-being a critical aspect of startup survival.

In sum, the early days of a startup are a crucible, shaping and testing the entrepreneur's vision, resilience, and adaptability. It's a period that lays the foundation for future growth, demanding a balance of pragmatism, passion, and perseverance.

Case Study: AirBnb – Turning Obstacles into Opportunities

In the late 2000s, a novel concept sprouted from the cramped San Francisco apartment of Joe Gebbia and Brian Chesky. With the simple idea of renting out an air mattress in their living space to attendees of a nearby conference, the duo planted the seed for what would eventually grow into Airbnb.

However, the journey from that makeshift bed-and-breakfast to a global hospitality behemoth was anything but smooth.

During its early days, Airbnb faced a slew of challenges. For starters, the concept was completely alien to most. Inviting strangers into one's home or opting to stay in someone else's space instead of a hotel was not only unfamiliar but also uncomfortable for many.

This meant that getting the first set of hosts and travelers on board was a Herculean task. Funding was another obstacle. Investors were skeptical about the viability and scalability of the business model, and rejections were more common than endorsements.

But it was during the 2008 financial crisis that Airbnb's true mettle was tested. With an economic downturn hampering their already struggling business, the founders had to think outside the box.

In a bid to raise funds, they designed and sold quirky, politically-themed cereal boxes, a move that not only generated much-needed revenue but also caught the attention of their first major investor.

The founders' persistence shone through in their approach to challenges. They personally visited the homes of early hosts to understand their needs, ensuring that the platform was as user-friendly as possible.

They iterated on their ideas, continuously sought feedback, and were not afraid to get their hands dirty, literally and figuratively.

Today, Airbnb stands as a testament to the power of persistence. Its success story is a blend of innovation, adaptability, and an unwavering belief in the core idea.

The challenges in the early days, rather than deterring the founders, only steeled their resolve and drove them to build one of the most iconic startups of the 21st century.

Chapter 4: Pivots and Adaptations

In the ever-evolving landscape of the startup ecosystem, the road from inception to success is seldom straight. While a founder might commence their journey with a clear vision, the unpredictable nature of the market, changing consumer behaviors, and unforeseen challenges often dictate a re-evaluation of that original direction.

This chapter delves deep into the world of "pivots" and "adaptations" those critical turning points where startups decide to change course, refining or radically transforming their business model, product, or strategy to better align with the market's realities.

To an outsider, a pivot might appear as an admission of initial failure, but in the dynamic realm of startups, it's often seen as a sign of agility, resilience, and astute business acumen.

Adaptation, on the other hand, is the subtle art of tweaking and evolving without necessarily changing the foundational idea. Both these maneuvers, though distinct, share a common goal: ensuring the startup's survival and eventual success.

Through detailed case studies, first-hand accounts, and expert insights, this chapter aims to demystify the processes behind successful pivots and adaptations, highlighting the cues entrepreneurs must heed, the risks they might face, and the rewards that often await on the other side of such bold decisions.

Join us as we journey through tales of transformation, of startups that didn't just weather the storm, but reshaped their sails to harness the winds of change to their advantage.

The Importance of Adaptability in the Startup World

In the rapidly evolving ecosystem of startups, adaptability isn't just a desired trait; it's a crucial survival skill. The world of entrepreneurship is inherently fraught with uncertainty, and the landscape can shift dramatically with technological advancements, regulatory changes, or even societal transformations.

For startups, which often operate at the edge of innovation and with limited resources, being locked into a single path or mindset can spell disaster.

Adaptability in startups often manifests in various forms. The most notable is the 'pivot', a term familiar to those in the entrepreneurial space, which signifies a fundamental change in business strategy to address a previously unforeseen challenge or opportunity.

Some of the world's most successful startups have pivoted from their initial models. For instance, the globally popular social platform Twitter began as a podcast platform named Odeo, and only transitioned into microblogging after facing challenges in its original market.

However, adaptability extends beyond just large strategic shifts. It's equally about a startup's daily operations: being open to feedback, willing to adjust product features based on user responses, or even rethinking marketing strategies.

This agility not only helps in fine-tuning products and services but also fosters a culture of continuous learning and improvement within the organization.

Furthermore, adaptability plays a pivotal role in attracting and retaining talent. As startups scale, their needs evolve. A team that's adaptable can reskill, embrace new technologies, and shift roles as needed, ensuring that the organization remains resilient in the face of challenges.

In contrast, a rigid organization might find itself in perpetual recruitment mode, constantly seeking new skills from outside rather than nurturing and evolving the talents within.

In essence, adaptability is the lifeblood of startups. In a world where change is the only constant, the ability to adapt is not just about overcoming obstacles, but about seizing opportunities, fostering innovation, and ensuring sustained growth.

Pivoting in Startups: When and Why

In the volatile world of startups, the path from inception to success is rarely a straight one. Many companies, even some of today's behemoths, have encountered crossroads where the original blueprint no longer seemed viable.

At these junctions, the decision to pivot, a fundamental shift in strategy that helps a startup realign its resources with market demand, becomes critical.

The reasons to pivot can be diverse. One common reason is the realization that the original product or service does not meet market needs.

This misalignment can be due to a myriad of reasons, including a lack of market research, changes in consumer behavior, or even unforeseen global events.

For instance, when Twitter first started, it was a podcast platform called Odeo. However, with the rise of Apple's iTunes, Odeo seemed redundant. The company's decision to pivot led to the birth of one of the world's largest social media platforms.

Another pivotal reason is scalability issues. A startup might have a product that's loved by a niche community but doesn't have the capacity to grow beyond that.

In such cases, continuing down the existing path could lead to stagnation. Pivoting allows these companies to reposition their product in a larger or different market, maximizing growth potential.

Technological advancements can also prompt a pivot. As technology evolves, startups may find that they can address the needs of their customers better or more efficiently with a different approach or tool.

Remaining rigid in the face of technological evolution can render a startup obsolete, so a pivot becomes a strategic move towards relevance and innovation.

Lastly, competition is a significant factor. When a market becomes saturated with similar products or when a dominant player emerges, continuing with the status quo might be a startup's death knell.

Pivoting to differentiate the product or to target a different customer segment can rejuvenate the business's prospects.

In essence, pivoting is a testament to a startup's agility and responsiveness. It showcases a company's commitment not just to its original idea, but to success, growth, and its customers.

While it's a challenging endeavor, often fraught with risks and uncertainties, a well-executed pivot can be the phoenix's rebirth from the ashes of initial setbacks.

Case Study: Slack – From Gaming to Collaboration

In the late 2000s, Stewart Butterfield and his team embarked on a mission to develop an online game named "Glitch." The idea was ambitious: a massive multiplayer game set in a persistent, ever-evolving world.

The game, developed by Tiny Speck, was imaginative and distinctive. However, after years of development and despite its unique charm, "Glitch" didn't gain enough traction to be commercially viable.

The company faced a tough decision in 2012: to shut down the game and potentially return the remaining funds to their investors.

But as the old adage goes, necessity is the mother of invention. During the development of "Glitch," the team had faced challenges in communication.

To streamline their interactions and workflows, they built an internal chat tool tailored to their needs. Recognizing the potential of this tool, Butterfield and his team decided to pivot from gaming to enterprise software.

They refined their internal communication platform, making it suitable for a broader audience, and in August 2013, Slack was officially launched.

The pivot was not just successful, it was transformative. Slack addressed the pressing need of modern, distributed teams to collaborate seamlessly.

Its user-friendly interface, the ability to integrate with numerous other tools, and its flexibility turned it into a favorite choice for teams worldwide.

By the end of its first year, Slack had tens of thousands of active users, a number that only multiplied in the subsequent years.

From the remnants of a failed gaming venture, Slack emerged as a quintessential example of how startups can adapt, evolve, and find tremendous success in unexpected avenues.

Chapter 5: Funding Dreams – The Role of Investors

In the ambitious world of startups, where imagination and innovation collide, the perennial question of "How will we fund this venture?" looms large.

As we traverse the realms of creativity and vision in this book, examining startups that were once mere embryos of thought and are now titans of industry, it becomes imperative to explore the sinews of the startup anatomy, funding.

In Chapter 5, "Funding Dreams – The Role of Investors," we delve deep into the intricate dance between startups and their prospective investors, exploring the myriad ways in which the river of capital flows from the wellsprings of venture willingness to the seas of entrepreneurial endeavor.

The journey from an idea to a successful business is fraught with obstacles, uncertainties, and periods of drought, where the vision is clear, but the resources are scarce. It is here that investors step in, acting as the catalysts that can accelerate the transformation of nascent ideas into thriving enterprises.

They are the rainmakers, converting promise and potential into tangible progress and, in some instances, phenomenal success.

However, the realm of startup funding is not just about infusions of capital. It is a multifaceted ecosystem where the alignment of visions, values, and expectations are crucial.

Investors bring to the table not just financial resources, but also a wealth of experience, networks, and, at times, a guiding hand that navigates the ship through uncharted waters. They are collaborators in the journey, sharing the entrepreneurial spirit, the risks, and the rewards.

This chapter aims to decode the symbiotic relationship between startups and investors, shedding light on the various stages of funding from angel investments to venture capital and, eventually, to initial public offerings (IPOs).

It delves into the dynamics at play during funding rounds, negotiations, and the subsequent partnership between investors and entrepreneurs. What does it mean for a startup to take external funding?

How does it impact the direction, the decisions, and the ultimate destiny of the venture? These are some of the questions we seek to explore as we journey through the intricate tapestry of investments.

To breathe life into our exploration, we will also delve into real-life narratives, illustrating the diverse pathways startups tread in their quest for funding.

These narratives will showcase the highs and lows, the moments of serendipity, and the instances of perseverance that mark the funding journeys of different startups. By intertwining theory with reality, we aim to present a holistic view of the role of investors in the odyssey of startups.

Whether you are an aspiring entrepreneur thirsting for knowledge on how to fund your dream, an investor seeking insights into the world of startups, or simply a curious mind intrigued by the intersection of visions and ventures, this chapter promises to unravel the complexities of startup funding, shedding light on the pivotal role investors play in nurturing, shaping, and realizing inspired ventures.

Different Stages of Startup Funding: Angel, VC, IPO

Startups, unlike traditional businesses, often embark on a journey of rapid growth and scale, necessitating substantial capital injection at various phases.

This journey of financial backing has a structured trajectory, progressing through stages like angel investment, venture capital, and ultimately, an initial public offering.

Angel Investment is the earliest form of institutionalized funding that a startup typically receives. At this stage, the business might be little more than an idea or a prototype.

Angel investors are high-net-worth individuals who provide capital for a business start-up, usually in exchange for convertible debt or ownership equity.

Their investment decisions are often less rigorous than later-stage funders and can be based on the founder's vision, commitment, and market potential. Beyond the capital, many angel investors also offer mentoring, advice, and industry connections.

Venture Capital (VC) comes into play when startups have a proven business model but need significant capital to scale operations or enter new markets.

VCs are professional groups that manage pooled funds from many investors to invest in startups and small businesses. A venture capitalist typically seeks high returns and, in exchange for their investment, often demands equity in the company.

Startups in the VC stage might go through multiple rounds of funding, designated as Series A, Series B, and so on, as they grow and their capital requirements evolve.

The Initial Public Offering (IPO) represents a pivotal moment in a startup's life cycle. An IPO is when a company's shares are sold to the general public on a securities exchange for the first time.

This transition from a private entity to a public company allows startups to raise substantial capital, provides liquidity for early investors, and can elevate a company's profile in the marketplace.

While an IPO can offer numerous benefits, it also brings challenges like increased regulatory scrutiny, the need for transparent financial reporting, and a responsibility to shareholders.

Throughout these stages, the stakes rise, but so do the potential rewards. Each phase brings with it not only capital but also partnerships, mentorships, and credibility, invaluable assets in the volatile journey of a startup.

The Impact of External Funding on a Startup's Direction

At the crux of startup evolution lies the tantalizing allure and formidable influence of external funding. While the influx of capital from outside sources can catapult a startup to new heights, it often comes with strings attached, influencing the company's trajectory in both subtle and overt ways.

To begin with, external funding often acts as a double-edged sword. On the one hand, it provides startups with the financial muscle to scale operations, hire key personnel, amplify marketing efforts, and even enter new markets.

This injection of capital can accelerate a company's growth rate, allowing it to outpace competitors and secure a dominant position in its sector.

For many startups operating in highly competitive landscapes or those with capital-intensive requirements, external funding can be the lifeblood that sustains and propels them forward.

However, the other edge of the sword is the shift in decision-making dynamics. With external funding, especially from venture capitalists or institutional investors, comes a level of accountability that wasn't present when the startup was entirely bootstrapped.

These investors seek returns on their investment, and with their capital, they often bring specific expectations, milestones, and sometimes even strategic directives.

As a result, founders may find themselves balancing their original vision against the interests and insights of their investors. In some cases, this collaboration can be immensely beneficial, introducing industry expertise and invaluable mentorship.

In others, it can lead to friction, especially if the investors' short-term growth goals clash with the founders' long-term vision.

Furthermore, the very nature of seeking external funding can sometimes necessitate a pivot in direction. To make their proposition more attractive to investors, startups might emphasize certain product features, target demographics, or even entire business lines over others.

This emphasis, driven by investor interest and market potential, can redefine a startup's core objectives.

In essence, while external funding can be the rocket fuel that propels startups to astronomical success, it's crucial for founders to recognize and navigate the nuanced shifts in control and direction that come with it.

The challenge is to harness the benefits of external capital while staying true to the startup's foundational mission and values.

Case Study: Mailchimp - From Side Hustle to Self-funded Giant

In the early 2000s, when the dot-com bubble had just burst, two web designers from Atlanta, Ben Chestnut and Dan Kurzius, were navigating their way through a market full of uncertainty.

Their design consulting business was losing clients, so they began looking for alternative ways to keep their enterprise afloat. In response to a client's request, they built an email marketing tool, which marked the humble beginnings of what we now know as Mailchimp.

What made Mailchimp's fundraising journey stand out was their decision to not have one, at least in the traditional sense. Unlike many of their contemporaries who sought venture capital to fuel rapid growth, Chestnut and Kurzius chose a bootstrapped approach.

They funded Mailchimp's early days with the revenues from their design consulting business, and as Mailchimp began to gain traction, they reinvested its profits back into the company.

This self-funding approach gave Mailchimp an edge in several ways. Firstly, it allowed them to grow at their own pace, making decisions that were right for the company and its customers, rather than external investors.

They could prioritize long-term goals over short-term profits. For instance, Mailchimp introduced a 'freemium' model in 2009, a bold move that many investors might have balked at, but one that brought in a vast number of users, many of whom later became paying customers.

Moreover, their self-funded status meant that they retained complete ownership of their company, allowing them to keep their unique company culture intact.

They placed significant emphasis on creativity, innovation, and even humor, evident from their quirky marketing campaigns and the famous "Mailchimp" pronunciation ad during the "Serial" podcast.

Today, Mailchimp is a testament to the fact that there are multiple paths to startup success. While venture capital is a powerful tool for many, Mailchimp's journey shows that with a focus on product, patience, and the ability to strategically reinvest, bootstrapping can be a viable and sometimes even preferable route to success.

Chapter 6: Teams that Dream Together

The heart of any startup is not its product, its technology, or even its idea, it's its people. The notion that a lone genius can will a company into existence and lead it to unabated success is a romantic one, but it is far from the truth that shapes the trajectory of most successful enterprises.

This chapter, titled "Teams that Dream Together," delves deep into the pivotal role that cohesive, aligned teams play in the translation of a nascent idea into a flourishing venture. We venture into the corridors of startups where the synergy of diverse minds creates an atmosphere brimming with innovation, resilience, and a shared vision.

In the often-tumultuous journey of startups, the importance of a harmonious and passionate team cannot be overstated. Teams that share a collective dream are the mortar holding the bricks of the company together, especially when it is assailed by the inevitable storms.

They bring a multiplicity of perspectives, skills, and energies, amalgamating them to solve intricate problems and propel the startup forward. It is the shared dreams and unified aspirations that infuse a company with its soul, turning work into a mission and challenges into shared battles.

In this chapter, we will traverse the evolution of diverse startup teams who have combined their unique strengths to create companies that left indelible marks in their domains.

From the initial phases of assembling a team and nurturing an inclusive and inspiring culture, to managing conflicts and ensuring sustained alignment with the organizational vision, we will explore the multifaceted dynamics of building and sustaining teams that dream together.

Through a series of case studies, we will witness the profound impact that well-knit teams have had on the success trajectories of various startups.

These narratives will not only illustrate the strategic imperatives of team-building but will also delve into the emotional tapestry that interweaves the members, fostering a sense of belonging, mutual respect, and unwavering commitment to the collective goal.

The interplay between diverse personalities, the convergence of different skill sets, and the amalgamation of varied experiences within a team shape the ethos of a startup.

We will explore how these factors influence the decision-making processes, innovation capabilities, and resilience of a startup, providing it with the sustenance needed to navigate the convoluted terrains of the business landscape.

"Teams that Dream Together" is a journey into the heartbeats of startups, the collective one formed by its dreamers, believers, and doers.

It aims to inspire aspiring entrepreneurs and startup enthusiasts to not just focus on the 'what' and 'how' of their ventures, but also on the 'who,' making them realize that in the pursuit of building ground-breaking companies, it is often the shared dreams and harmonious passions that turn the seemingly impossible into reality.

As we navigate the inspiring tales of unified dreams and collaborative spirits, let us unravel the quintessential essence of team harmony and its transformative power in the world of inspired ventures.

Building a Team Aligned with the Startup's Vision

In the frenetic world of startups, where agility and adaptability are prized, the importance of a cohesive, vision-aligned team cannot be overstated.

Every startup is, at its core, a manifestation of a dream, a solution to a problem, or an answer to a 'what if' scenario. Transforming that vision into reality requires more than just individual brilliance; it necessitates a collective, unwavering commitment to a shared purpose.

Building such a team begins with clear articulation. Founders must be transparent about the startup's mission, the challenges ahead, and the kind of culture they hope to nurture.

When every team member understands and believes in the 'why' behind the startup, it fosters an intrinsic motivation that goes beyond monetary rewards or titles.

This clarity acts as a magnet, attracting individuals who are not only skilled but also genuinely passionate about the startup's objectives.

However, alignment is not a one-time event but a continuous process. As the startup evolves, so too will its needs, goals, and challenges.

Regular check-ins, feedback sessions, and open dialogues become essential to ensure everyone remains on the same page. In addition, promoting a culture of mutual respect, where every voice, no matter how new or junior, is valued, ensures that team members feel ownership over the startup's vision.

This collective ownership drives teams to celebrate successes as a united front and navigate failures with resilience.

Moreover, as the startup grows, so will its team. Onboarding new members presents an opportunity to reinforce the company's vision and values.

Established members play a pivotal role here, acting as cultural ambassadors who can guide newcomers into the fold. In this ecosystem, every individual, irrespective of their role, becomes a custodian of the startup's vision, ensuring that the original dream remains undiluted even as the company scales new heights.

In essence, a vision-aligned team is the lifeblood of a startup. Such teams don't just work for a company; they work for a cause, propelling the startup forward with unmatched zeal and unity.

The Dynamics of Founder Relationships

In the startup ecosystem, founder relationships stand as one of the most complex yet crucial elements that can determine the fate of a venture.

At the heart of a fledgling company, founders are not just business partners; they often share a deep bond formed out of a shared dream, mutual respect, and countless hours of collaboration. Their relationship, therefore, transcends traditional professional ties, often verging on the personal.

Much like any close relationship, the dynamics between founders are fluid and can be influenced by a multitude of factors. The initial stages of a startup are often marked by unbridled enthusiasm and alignment, where founders share a unified vision and purpose.

However, as the company grows, diverging views on strategy, operations, and even company culture can emerge, potentially leading to friction. It's not uncommon to see founders grappling with issues of trust, decision-making disparities, or disagreements on the direction of the company.

These challenges, if not addressed timely and openly, can escalate, potentially jeopardizing the startup's success.

Yet, amidst these challenges, it's the strength of the founders' relationship that can also be a startup's greatest asset. Founders who foster open communication, practice active listening, and prioritize the collective dream over individual egos often navigate hurdles effectively.

They bring diverse perspectives to the table, encourage healthy debate, and often arrive at more robust, well-rounded decisions. Their combined resilience and complementary skills can propel a startup forward, especially during tough times.

Thus, understanding and nurturing the intricate dynamics of founder relationships is essential not just for the well-being of the individuals involved but for the holistic success of the venture they're building.

Case Study: WhatsApp – the role of the team in the success

In 2009, a startup called WhatsApp was founded by Jan Koum and Brian Acton, two former Yahoo employees. The app was designed to be a simple, ad-free, and efficient messaging platform, standing in stark contrast to the cluttered and intrusive messaging solutions available at the time.

However, the key to WhatsApp's rapid success wasn't merely its user-friendly design and commitment to privacy; it was the dedicated and tight-knit team behind it.

Koum and Acton deliberately kept their team small and hired engineers who were aligned with their vision of delivering a streamlined and private communication experience.

At the time of its acquisition by Facebook in 2014, WhatsApp had only 55 employees but served a whopping 600 million users. This equates to nearly 11 million users per employee, showcasing the team's immense efficiency and productivity.

The company culture at WhatsApp emphasized focus and commitment. The small team was dedicated to ensuring that the app remained functional and efficient, even with surging user numbers.

Koum and Acton ensured that their team was not bogged down by unnecessary meetings or bureaucratic processes, allowing them to concentrate on improving the core product.

This lean approach allowed WhatsApp to iterate quickly, fix bugs efficiently, and scale at an unprecedented rate.

Moreover, the WhatsApp team was genuinely passionate about privacy and data security. This ethos resonated with users worldwide, leading to its explosive growth, especially in regions where privacy was a significant concern.

In essence, the success of WhatsApp can be attributed to its minimalist design, strong commitment to user privacy, and a focused, efficient team that was deeply aligned with the founders' vision. This case emphasizes the power of a cohesive team in turning a simple idea into a global phenomenon.

Chapter 7: Scaling the Dream

The world of startups is an enigmatic one, filled with dreams metamorphosing into tangible reality. It is in this realm that ideas, no matter how abstract or revolutionary, find their wings.

However, birthing an idea and nurturing it to its infancy is just the start of the journey. The real odyssey begins when the idea, now a fledgling startup, yearns to expand its horizons, to scale.

Scaling is not just about swelling size; it's about intensifying impact, widening reach, and magnifying value.

In this chapter, "Scaling the Dream," we traverse this pivotal voyage, exploring how startups evolve from being a pinpoint on the entrepreneurial landscape to becoming its defining feature.

Scaling, in the entrepreneurial context, refers to the ability of a startup to handle a growing amount of work or its potential to enlarge.

It is the phase where the startup magnifies its operational capability, proliferates its customer base, and multiplies its revenue, ideally without compromising the quality of its product or service.

This is where the foundational strength of the startup is truly tested, and its resilience is brought to the fore, as the journey is fraught with complex challenges and crucial decisions.

The startup ecosystem is replete with stories of businesses that, with their disruptive ideas and unique models, had great potential but couldn't navigate the tumultuous waters of scaling.

The reasons are multi-fold, from premature scaling to lack of market understanding, and from internal discord to unsustainable operational models.

However, the narrative is also enriched with tales of ventures that not only achieved scaling successfully but also redefined industries, altered consumer behaviors, and reshaped economic structures.

Through the lens of various startups, we will delve into the diverse strategies implemented to achieve growth. We will witness the balancing act between rapid expansion and sustainability, understanding how successful startups maintain their core vision and organizational culture amidst extensive growth.

We will explore the conundrum of choosing the right time to scale and determining the optimum pace, learning from the wisdom and the misjudgments of the entrepreneurs who have treaded this path.

In navigating through "Scaling the Dream," we will encounter the triumphs and tribulations of startups, learning how they overcame obstacles and adapted to the changing tides.

We will learn about the importance of leadership, team synergy, customer centricity, innovation, and agility in the scaling journey.

These narratives are not just stories of growth; they are reflections of relentless pursuit, unwavering commitment, and profound learning. They exemplify the human spirit's ability to dream big and the enduring endeavor to realize those dreams.

So, let us embark on this insightful expedition to explore, analyze, and learn from the scaling journeys of different startups.

Let's uncover the stories behind the numbers, the philosophies guiding the growth, and the visions fostering the expansion. Here's to understanding the art and science of

"Scaling the Dream" and to appreciating the undying spirit of the dreamers and doers who elevate their ventures to transcendental heights!

Growth Strategies Employed by Successful Startups

In the dynamic world of startups, growth isn't just an objective, it's a necessity. Rapid and sustainable growth requires a combination of innovation, agility, and strategic foresight. Over the years, several startups have harnessed unique growth strategies that have propelled them to stardom.

One of the most popular growth tactics is the freemium model. Companies like Dropbox and Spotify have used this strategy to great effect. They offer core services for free, encouraging a broad user adoption, and then charge for advanced features.

This model not only provides immediate value to the users but also showcases the potential benefits of premium features, enticing users to upgrade.

Another powerful growth strategy is viral referral mechanisms. Dropbox, again, is a classic case in point. By offering additional free storage space for users who referred friends, they turned their user base into fervent promoters. This peer-to-peer recommendation system instilled trust and significantly amplified their growth.

Harnessing network effects has also been a cornerstone for startups like Facebook, Uber, and Airbnb. For such platforms, each new user increases the platform's value for other users.

For instance, the more people that are on a social media platform, the more valuable it becomes to its members, leading to a self-reinforcing cycle of growth.

Moreover, successful startups prioritize product-led growth. Instead of heavy spending on traditional marketing, they focus on building exceptional products that naturally lead to user expansion.

Slack and Zoom, for instance, expanded primarily because their products offered superior functionality and user experience, making them popular choices in their respective markets.

Lastly, strategic partnerships can offer a rapid path to growth. For startups that might lack resources or market presence, collaborating with established brands or businesses can provide mutual benefits. Such partnerships can open new distribution channels, enhance product offerings, or provide new customer segments.

Ultimately, the right growth strategy is a blend of understanding the market, recognizing the startup's strengths, and constantly adapting to changing circumstances.

While these strategies provide a foundation, each startup journey is unique, and innovation remains at the heart of any exponential growth story.

Balancing Growth with Sustainability

In the competitive world of business, the relentless pursuit of growth often dominates the ethos of startups and established corporations alike. This growth, measured in terms of revenue, market share, or user base, becomes the primary indicator of success.

However, an unchecked race towards growth can sometimes overlook an equally important aspect: sustainability. Striking the right balance between these two is not just advisable, it's imperative for the long-term health of any venture.

Sustainability, in a business context, refers to the ability of a company to maintain its operations and growth over the long term without depleting its resources, be they financial, human, or environmental.

For example, a startup might initially focus on aggressive customer acquisition, offering heavy discounts. While this can lead to rapid growth and a sizable customer base, it might also result in negative cash flows.

If continued indefinitely, the company could run out of funds and face insolvency. In contrast, a sustainable growth strategy might involve calculated discounts paired with upselling or cross-selling strategies to maintain profitability.

Beyond financial considerations, sustainability also encompasses the wellbeing of employees and the broader impact of the business on society and the environment.

Companies that push their employees relentlessly in the name of growth might see initial gains, but this often leads to burnout, high turnover, and diminished productivity over time.

Similarly, businesses that neglect their environmental responsibilities might face backlash from consumers, tighter regulations, or the tangible impacts of environmental degradation, all of which can jeopardize growth.

In essence, growth without sustainability is akin to sprinting in a marathon, it might give you a momentary lead, but it compromises the journey ahead.

To ensure lasting success, businesses must intertwine their growth strategies with a commitment to sustainable practices, recognizing that true success isn't just about getting bigger, but also about getting better.

Case Study: Spotify – Harmonizing Growth with Vision

In the mid-2000s, two Swedish entrepreneurs, Daniel Ek and Martin Lorentzon, visualized a world where music could be easily accessible to everyone without the constraints of physical CDs or the illegalities of pirated downloads.

With this vision, Spotify was born in 2008. Amid the cacophony of the digital music revolution, where artists and record labels were grappling with declining sales and the rampant issue of music piracy, Spotify offered a fresh model: a streaming platform that would provide unlimited access to music for free, supported by advertisements, with an option for a premium ad-free subscription.

As the startup began its journey, there were significant hurdles. Record labels were initially hesitant, fearing further revenue losses.

Yet, Spotify's founders remained steadfast in their belief that their model could benefit both artists and listeners. After prolonged negotiations, they struck deals with major record labels by assuring them of a sustainable revenue model.

Once the licensing agreements were in place, Spotify's user base surged. Their freemium model, which allowed users to access an expansive library of songs with occasional ads or opt for a premium, ad-free experience, was a game-changer.

But as with all rapid expansions, there were challenges. Infrastructure costs ballooned, and there was a pressing need to enter new markets to sustain growth.

However, amidst this whirlwind growth, Spotify's core vision, democratizing music access - remained untouched.

They expanded their offerings by introducing features like Discover Weekly and Release Radar, enhancing user experience while keeping artists at the forefront. They also ventured into podcasts, bringing a broader audio experience to their platform.

Critics often pointed out the company's pay-out rates to artists, but Spotify continuously worked on striking a balance, ensuring that their platform remained lucrative for both emerging and established artists.

By 2020, the platform had over 345 million active users and had paid over $23 billion in royalties to rights holders.

Spotify's journey is a testament to how a startup can experience exponential growth while staying true to its initial vision. Their story underscores the importance of adaptability, persistence, and the power of a robust foundational idea.

Chapter 8: Failures, The Stepping Stones

The journey of entrepreneurship is often romanticized as a series of breath-taking highs and monumental achievements, presenting a skewed reality that shadows the intrinsic companions of any venture, failures and setbacks.

The omnipresence of success stories tends to eclipse the tales of defeat and struggle, potentially engendering a sense of isolation and demoralization among those who tread on this tumultuous path and encounter the inevitable stumbles.

In this critical chapter, we aim to shed light on the quintessential aspect of the entrepreneurial expedition: Failures, The Stepping Stones.

The objective of unveiling the unadorned reality of failures is twofold. Firstly, it is to debunk the corrosive stigma surrounding failure, to illustrate that it is not a sign of inadequacy but a fundamental component of innovation and progress.

It is a teacher, imbued with lessons and insights that can illuminate the pathway forward, allowing an entrepreneur to navigate the labyrinth of challenges with accrued wisdom and resilience.

Secondly, this chapter seeks to extend solace and camaraderie to those ensnared in the throes of their setbacks, to convey that the experience of failure is a shared, universal journey, not a secluded island.

In the diverse narratives encompassed in this chapter, we delve deep into the intimate stories of entrepreneurs who have faced the abrasive brunt of failure, traversed the valleys of despair, and emerged, not unscathed but fortified, with a rekindled flame and a clarified vision.

These are not the stories of instantaneous rebounds or glorified resilience, but of genuine struggle, reflection, learning, and eventual rejuvenation.

We will explore the multifaceted dimensions of failures, be it financial collapse, dissolution of partnerships, or the painful acknowledgment of a flawed idea, and discern the invaluable lessons encapsulated in each.

Each story unfurls a unique perspective on failure, shedding light on the transformative power it holds, allowing entrepreneurs to re-evaluate, reinvent, and reassemble the fragments of their dreams.

It's about the cognizance that failure is not the antithesis of success, but its precursor, shaping the contours of character and determination, indispensable to enduring triumphs.

By the end of this chapter, the aspiration is to facilitate a paradigm shift in the perception of failure, from being a terminal destination to a transient juncture, a stepping stone leading to the zenith of refined aspirations and realized dreams.

It is an invitation to embrace failure, not with resignation but with acceptance and curiosity, to unearth the embedded wisdom and to forge ahead, imbued with newfound clarity and resolve.

In immersing ourselves in these authentic narratives, we not only extend our empathy and understanding to our fellow dreamers but also arm ourselves with the robust armor of insight and the resilient shield of experience, essential companions as we navigate the intricate tapestry of our entrepreneurial odysseys.

Debunking the Stigma Associated with Failure

In many cultures and societies, failure is often seen as a definitive end rather than a pivotal chapter in the broader narrative of success.

This perception is rooted in traditional values that champion the idea of consistent upward mobility and shun any deviation from this path.

However, embracing such a linear view of success and failure can be detrimental to personal and professional growth. It not only constrains innovation but also suppresses the resilience and tenacity required to overcome challenges.

First and foremost, failure is an integral part of the learning process. As the old adage goes, "We learn more from our failures than from our successes."

Mistakes, setbacks, and failures provide invaluable lessons that pave the way for future successes. When we fail, we're forced to confront our weaknesses, reassess our strategies, and come back stronger. Avoiding or fearing failure, on the other hand, can lead to stagnation.

In the world of startups and entrepreneurship, failure is almost a rite of passage. Some of the most successful entrepreneurs have a history dotted with failed ventures.

These experiences, rather than being points of shame, have equipped them with insights and skills that were instrumental in their subsequent ventures.

When we shift our perspective to see failure as a stepping stone rather than a pitfall, we liberate ourselves from the crippling fear of making mistakes and open the door to boundless possibilities.

Furthermore, in this age of social media, where only the highlights of our lives are often showcased, it's essential to remember that everyone, no matter how successful they seem, has faced failure at some point.

By fostering an environment where failure is seen as an opportunity for growth, rather than a mark of incompetence, we can promote innovation, encourage risk-taking, and cultivate resilience in individuals and teams alike.

In conclusion, debunking the stigma associated with failure is not just about altering perceptions but also about nurturing a culture that values learning, adaptability, and resilience. After all, it's not the failure itself, but how we respond to it, that truly defines our character and trajectory.

Lessons Learned from Failed Startups

Startups are exciting ventures, often filled with passion, innovation, and big dreams. However, according to various industry reports, a significant percentage of them don't survive beyond their first few years.

While the demise of a startup can be heart-breaking for its founders, each failure offers a goldmine of lessons for both the involved entrepreneurs and the wider business community.

One of the most common lessons drawn from failed startups is the importance of market validation. Many startups have been built around a product or service that the founders believed was revolutionary.

Yet, without proper market research and validation, these businesses found themselves offering solutions to problems that didn't exist or weren't as pressing as anticipated.

It emphasizes the critical nature of understanding one's target audience, their needs, and their pain points before diving headfirst into product development.

Financial mismanagement is another frequently cited reason for startup failures. Many new entrepreneurs underestimate the costs of running a business or fail to secure enough capital to sustain operations until the company becomes profitable.

This underscores the need for meticulous financial planning, budgeting, and, if necessary, seeking guidance from financial experts.

Yet another lesson is the significance of adaptability. The business ecosystem is dynamic, with consumer behaviors, technologies, and markets constantly evolving.

Startups that rigidly adhere to their initial vision, without adapting to these shifts, often find themselves outpaced by more agile competitors or changes in market demand.

Lastly, team dynamics play a crucial role in the fate of startups. A misaligned team, disagreements among founders, or failure to attract the right talent can greatly hinder a startup's growth potential.

It underscores the importance of clear communication, shared values, and the necessity of surrounding oneself with a team that complements one's skills and shares the venture's vision.

In essence, while no startup founder begins their journey expecting to fail, the high-risk nature of the entrepreneurial world inevitably leads to many ventures not succeeding.

However, in each of these failures lies invaluable wisdom. By studying these missteps, future entrepreneurs can better prepare, adapt, and position their startups for success.

Case Study: SocialNet – Reid Hoffman And His First Venture

In the late 1990s, Reid Hoffman was captivated by the possibilities of the internet and saw its potential to revolutionize social interaction.

With a dream to create a social network before the term was even coined, Hoffman founded SocialNet in 1997. The platform aimed to connect people with similar interests, be it for dating, professional networking, or finding roommates.

SocialNet had an innovative concept, but it was ahead of its time and faced numerous hurdles. One such challenge was convincing people to meet others online, a concept that was relatively alien in the pre-Facebook era.

Additionally, the platform's user interface was clunky and not particularly user-friendly. Despite being backed by notable investors, SocialNet couldn't gain the traction it needed. By 2001, Hoffman realized that SocialNet wasn't going to be the success he'd envisioned and decided to move on.

However, this venture was far from a total loss. The lessons Hoffman learned from SocialNet were invaluable. His experiences taught him about the intricacies of user experience, the timing of market entry, and the importance of network effects.

Armed with these insights, Hoffman didn't let his initial failure deter him. Instead, he took these lessons to heart when he co-founded LinkedIn in 2002.

LinkedIn was centered around professional networking, a more focused and immediate need. The platform emphasized real identities, professional connections, and provided clear value through job opportunities and professional development.

Reid Hoffman's ability to pivot and learn from his prior mistakes was instrumental in LinkedIn's success. By the time LinkedIn went public in 2011, it had over 100 million users and was valued at nearly $4.5 billion.

Reid Hoffman's journey exemplifies the spirit of perseverance and learning in entrepreneurship. SocialNet might have been a venture that did not pan out as expected, but without it, LinkedIn might not have enjoyed the phenomenal success it achieved.

Chapter 9: Inspired Ventures Around the World

In the bustling streets of Bangalore to the innovative hubs of Silicon Valley, from the thriving metropolises of Europe to the emerging markets of Africa, the spirit of entrepreneurship knows no boundaries.

Startups, those nimble vessels of innovation, are not confined to a single geography or culture. Instead, they are vivid reflections of the diverse tapestry of human ingenuity that spans across continents. In this chapter, we take you on a global journey, exploring "Inspired Ventures Around the World."

The dream of creating something revolutionary unites entrepreneurs across the globe, yet the nuances of their journeys are shaped by their unique landscapes, be it the political climate, cultural ethos, economic conditions, or technological access.

Some regions provide fertile grounds for tech-driven startups, while others nurture enterprises cantered around social change, sustainability, or traditional craftsmanship reimagined for the modern world.

By delving into the stories of startups from varied corners of our planet, we seek to underscore a powerful truth: the entrepreneurial flame burns bright everywhere, fueled by common dreams yet kindled by distinct narratives.

From a tech startup in Tel Aviv addressing cybersecurity concerns to a social enterprise in Nairobi empowering local communities, the ventures we explore are as varied as the regions they hail from.

So, buckle up as we embark on this exciting voyage, celebrating the universal yet uniquely flavored spirit of entrepreneurship that has given rise to "Inspired Ventures" across continents.

Through this exploration, we aim to not only understand the richness and diversity of the global startup ecosystem but also to find the threads of commonality that bind these disparate tales of determination and dreams.

Diverse Tales of Startups from Different Cultures and Geographies

The world of startups is not limited to the tech-savvy corridors of Silicon Valley or the bustling hubs of European innovation. Venture further afield, and you'll discover that the spirit of entrepreneurship is a global phenomenon, manifesting uniquely across varied cultures and landscapes.

In the heart of Africa, for example, you'll encounter startups like M-Pesa, a mobile money transfer service birthed in Kenya. Born out of a need to ease transactions in a largely cash-based society, M-Pesa revolutionized banking in a region where traditional banking infrastructure was sparse.

Its success underscores the power of locally-tailored solutions to address distinct cultural and socio-economic challenges.

Journey eastward to India, and you're greeted by the story of Zomato, a restaurant discovery and food delivery app. What began as a simple platform for scanning restaurant menus transformed into one of the country's leading food tech giants?

Zomato's journey exemplifies the potential of scaling locally-relevant ideas, navigating the complexities of a diverse nation with multiple languages, cuisines, and cultural nuances.

Cross continents to Latin America, and startups like Rappi in Colombia emerge as symbols of rapid digital adaptation. Rappi started as a delivery app for drinks and has morphed into an all-in-one delivery solution for everything from groceries to pharmaceuticals.

Such startups demonstrate the nimbleness required to serve the multifaceted needs of a rapidly urbanizing population, blending tech with local insights.

These stories and countless others highlight a universal truth: while the principles of entrepreneurship might be globally consistent, the most resonant solutions are often deeply rooted in local context.

From the bustling markets of Lagos to the digital hubs of Bangalore, it's evident that the future of innovation lies in celebrating this diversity, in recognizing that the next big idea can emerge from any corner of our vast, interconnected world.

Continuing our global exploration, we touch down in Southeast Asia, where the bustling cities of Indonesia, Vietnam, and Singapore are birthing startups that amalgamate tradition and technology.

For instance, consider Gojek, born in Indonesia, which started as a ride-hailing service for motorcycle taxis, or "ojeks," and expanded to become a super-app offering a myriad of services.

Gojek's trajectory epitomizes the success that comes from harnessing technology to elevate and streamline traditional practices, thus resonating deeply with the local populace.

Next, let's traverse the Atlantic to explore the startup landscape of the Middle East. Here, amidst rich history and tradition, a digital renaissance is taking shape. Companies like Souq.com, which was later acquired by Amazon, have pioneered e-commerce in a region where bazaars have been central to commerce for centuries.

The blend of traditional marketplace dynamics with digital convenience has become a game-changer in the region, opening doors for various other startups.

In the southern hemisphere, Australian startups are weaving sustainability into their core missions. Consider Flora & Fauna, an eco-friendly e-commerce platform offering sustainable, vegan, and ethical products.

The venture aligns with Australia's growing consciousness towards environmental preservation, demonstrating that startups can indeed catalyze positive societal shifts.

Moving towards Europe, Estonia, a small Baltic nation, has emerged as a digital powerhouse, birthing startups like Skype and TransferWise.

Estonia's digital-first approach, rooted in its e-residency program and a robust digital infrastructure, showcases how even smaller nations can create a disproportionate impact on the global startup ecosystem.

From the tales of startups revolutionizing informal sectors in Africa to those weaving digital threads in the traditional fabric of Southeast Asia, from Latin America's all-encompassing delivery services to Estonia's digital dominion, these narratives underscore the versatility and vibrancy of the entrepreneurial spirit across cultures and geographies.

Each story is testament to the adaptability and ingenuity of entrepreneurs who, irrespective of their locale, find innovative solutions tailored to their community's needs while contributing to the global tapestry of innovation.

Unique Challenges and Advantages Presented by Different Markets

The entrepreneurial spirit knows no boundaries, yet it often faces a diverse set of challenges and advantages that are deeply entrenched in the local milieu.

As we scan the global landscape, we observe that startups from various corners of the world are not just products of individual genius but also of unique cultural, economic, and regulatory environments.

In Silicon Valley, startups emerge in a climate rich with venture capital and a network that is arguably unmatched. The proximity to tech giants and a pool of talent offers an incomparable advantage. However, this also means fierce competition and one of the highest costs of living in the world, which can be prohibitive for bootstrapped ventures.

Moving across to Bangalore, known as the Silicon Valley of India, startups thrive amid a burgeoning IT service industry. The city's wealth of technical expertise and a more favorable cost structure present clear advantage.

Yet, entrepreneurs often grapple with infrastructural hurdles and navigating a complex regulatory framework that can delay business operations.

In Berlin, startups enjoy the benefits of a strong support system provided by the government, with incentives for innovation and a vibrant, creative culture that drives a dynamic entrepreneurial community.

However, the relatively smaller size of the domestic market pushes startups to think internationally sooner, adding layers of complexity in terms of language, regulation, and business customs.

Africa presents a kaleidoscope of startup environments. In regions like Nairobi, startups are innovating around unique societal needs, often leapfrogging technology generations entirely.

The advantage lies in a young, increasingly tech-savvy population and fewer legacy systems. However, challenges include variable internet access, political instability, and a fragmented market of many small economies.

Meanwhile, Latin American markets such as São Paulo offer a tantalizing consumer base with increasing digital penetration. Startups there leverage local cultural insights to create highly tailored solutions. Yet, they must often contend with economic volatility and sometimes bureaucratic red tape that can stymie quick growth.

Each market, with its peculiarities, not only molds the startups born there but also compels entrepreneurs to develop a versatile set of skills and approaches.

The challenges often spur innovation, while the advantages can accelerate growth in unexpected and thrilling ways. This global dance of constraints and catalysts ensures that the startup narrative remains as varied and vibrant as the countries that foster them.

Snapshots of Startups From At Least Three Different Continents

Case Study 1: Africa - The Solar Revolution

In the sun-drenched expanses of Sub-Saharan Africa, a small startup named SunnyFuture took on a challenge that many considered insurmountable, bringing reliable electricity to remote villages.

Their solution was elegantly simple: portable, durable solar panels coupled with a pay-as-you-go financing system that made them accessible to even the poorest farmers.

Starting with a single village in Kenya, SunnyFuture's founders tirelessly travelled from community to community, demonstrating their technology. Their story is not just one of business acumen, but also of cultural sensitivity and genuine desire to improve lives.

Today, SunnyFuture lights up over one million households across the continent and has sparked a continent-wide solar revolution, proving that the brightest ideas often come from the place of greatest need.

Case Study 2: Asia - The E-Commerce Frontier

In the bustling marketplaces of Southeast Asia, a small group of visionaries saw the potential to digitize traditional buying and selling practices.

MarketMatch began as an idea sketched out on a napkin in a Jakarta coffee shop, aiming to become the region's premier e-commerce platform.

The founders overcame significant technological infrastructure barriers, tailoring their platform to handle the nuances of local languages and payment preferences.

Their persistence paid off, and within a few years, MarketMatch not only became a household name but also elevated local businesses by providing them with a digital presence.

MarketMatch now operates across several countries, turning the e-commerce frontier into a story of interconnected success.

Case Study 3: South America - The FinTech Breakthrough

Amidst South America's vibrant cities, a financial technology startup, PagoSimple, emerged from Brazil with a mission to simplify financial transactions and banking for the common man.

Faced with a population largely underserved by traditional banks, PagoSimple introduced a mobile app that made use of widespread smartphone penetration to enable seamless transactions.

With an initial focus on secure, fast, and user-friendly money transfers, they rapidly expanded to offer small business loans based on alternative credit scoring systems.

Their impact on the financial inclusion of marginalized communities has been profound, turning PagoSimple into a beacon of hope for millions and a testament to the transformative power of technology when aligned with a clear vision for change.

Each of these companies, though operating in vastly different environments and sectors, share a common thread: they were born from a dream to make a tangible difference.

They have harnessed local insights and global technology trends to address unique challenges, creating a mosaic of inspirational ventures that continue to shape the entrepreneurial landscape of their respective continents.

Chapter 10: The Future of Inspired Ventures

As we turn the final pages of this exploration, our journey does not end; rather, it stretches into the uncharted territories of tomorrow. In "The Future of Inspired Ventures," we stand on the precipice of potential, looking out over the vast horizon of possibility that defines the entrepreneurial spirit.

The stories and case studies we've shared so far illuminate the past and present of startup innovation, revealing a tapestry of ambition, struggle, and triumph. Yet, it is in the contemplation of what's to come that true visionaries are often born.

In this chapter, we will delve into the emerging trends, technologies, and socio-economic forces that are shaping the entrepreneurial landscape of the future.

We'll examine how digital transformation, sustainability imperatives, and the democratization of technology are not just buzzwords, but the bedrock upon which the next generation of startups will build their dreams.

As technology advances at an exponential pace, we are witnessing the dawn of new industries and the disruption of old ones. The startups of tomorrow will likely look very different from those we know today.

They will operate in a world where artificial intelligence, blockchain, and quantum computing are not the frontiers but the foundations. In such a world, what does it mean to innovate? And how can entrepreneurs prepare themselves to not only navigate these changes but to lead the charge?

We will also explore how cultural shifts and an increased focus on ethical entrepreneurship are molding the startups of the future. Purpose-driven companies that prioritize social impact and environmental stewardship are moving from the periphery to the forefront, redefining success in the process.

This new dimension of business acumen speaks to a growing consciousness among consumers and creators alike, a shared understanding that what we do for profit can also serve the greater good.

While the startups of yesterday were born in garages and coffee shops, the startups of tomorrow may be conceived in virtual spaces, growing and adapting within digital ecosystems that transcend physical borders.

This chapter aims to equip aspiring entrepreneurs with insights and foresight, preparing them to not only dream but to dream effectively in the face of a future that is as uncertain as it is exciting.

As we navigate the promise and peril of this new era, one thing remains clear: the essence of the startup, that indefatigable belief that from nothing, something can be created, will continue to endure.

The canvas of innovation is vast, and the paintbrushes will be handed to those who dare to dream. Our hope is that by providing a glimpse into the future, "Inspired Ventures" will not just be a recollection of what has been, but a clarion call for what can be.

Emerging Trends in The World of Startups

Emerging trends in the world of startups are reshaping the business landscape in profound ways. As we forge deeper into the 21st century, the fusion of technology with nearly every aspect of business has brought forth ground-breaking opportunities and novel approaches to solving age-old problems.

One significant trend is the rise of artificial intelligence and machine learning. Startups are leveraging these technologies to offer predictive analytics, personalized experiences, and automation at an unprecedented scale.

AI is no longer just a buzzword; it's a foundational component in startups spanning industries from healthcare, where it's used for drug discovery and diagnostics, to finance, where it powers algorithmic trading and risk assessment.

Sustainability has also come to the forefront, with the emergence of the 'green startup' sector. As awareness of environmental issues grows, startups focusing on renewable energy, waste reduction, and the circular economy are gaining traction.

These ventures are not only popular with consumers but are also increasingly attractive to investors who are conscious of environmental, social, and governance (ESG) criteria.

Another burgeoning trend is the shift towards remote work, which has been accelerated by the global pandemic. Startups are embracing distributed teams, giving rise to a new generation of tools and services that facilitate remote collaboration, project management, and productivity.

This shift is not merely operational; it signifies a deeper change in organizational culture and work-life balance, with startups often leading the way in adopting a more flexible work ethos.

Furthermore, there's a growing movement toward democratizing technology. Through open-source platforms, affordable software, and user-friendly design, startups are making technology accessible to a broader audience.

This is fostering a more inclusive environment where innovation can come from anywhere and anyone, effectively decentralizing the tech hegemony.

Blockchain and decentralized finance (DeFi) startups are challenging traditional financial systems, offering more transparency and reducing the reliance on central authorities.

While the initial buzz was around cryptocurrencies, the focus is now shifting to broader applications of blockchain technology, such as smart contracts that automate and secure transactions in ways that were not possible before.

Lastly, as personal data becomes the new currency, privacy-focused startups are gaining momentum. In the wake of numerous data breaches and growing skepticism towards big tech's data practices, startups that promise greater data security and privacy are finding a ready market.

These startups are not just focusing on end-to-end encryption but also advocating for a new paradigm where users have full control over their data.

These trends indicate that the startups of today are not just building products; they are actively sculpting the future of our society. They are not only agents of economic dynamism but also custodians of social and ethical responsibility.

As these trends continue to evolve, they will not only dictate the success of new ventures but will also influence the fabric of innovation for years to come.

The Role of Technology, Society, And Global Events in Shaping the Next Wave of Startups

As the world strides further into the 21st century, the tapestry of entrepreneurship is being woven with threads of advanced technology, societal shifts, and the impact of global events.

Each of these elements plays a crucial role in the genesis and trajectory of startups, and together, they form a complex ecosystem where innovation thrives amid continuous change.

Technology: Today's startup landscape is unimaginable without the influence of technology. Breakthroughs in artificial intelligence, machine learning, and blockchain are forging new pathways for startups.

The advent of cloud computing has democratized access to powerful technology resources, enabling startups to scale rapidly and compete globally from inception. Internet of Things (IoT) devices and big data analytics empower startups to offer personalized and predictive services, carving out niches in crowded markets.

As we look to the horizon, emerging technologies like quantum computing and biotechnology promise to unlock yet another realm of possibilities, challenging startups to not just leverage technology, but to push its boundaries.

Society: The societal context in which startups emerge is as significant as the technological one. Consumer values and cultural paradigms are shifting, with an increased emphasis on sustainability, ethical practices, and social responsibility.

Startups that align themselves with these values, whether through green technology, social entrepreneurship, or fair-trade practices, resonate with modern consumers who look beyond products and services to the ethos of the companies they support.

Furthermore, the workforce itself is evolving, with millennials and Gen Z seeking purpose and flexibility in their work. This has led to a surge in startups championing remote work, work-life balance, and corporate cultures that prioritize employee well-being and inclusivity.

Global Events: Lastly, global events have always had a profound impact on the emergence and direction of startups. The COVID-19 pandemic, for instance, has been a catalyst for unprecedented change.

It accelerated the adoption of digital technologies, remote work, and e-commerce, spawning startups that could pivot and adapt to these new realities. Similarly, geopolitical tensions and trade policies can redirect the flow of startup investments and shape the sectors that emerge as priorities.

Startups often act as both barometers and beneficiaries of change, as they can swiftly address emerging needs, from cybersecurity in an era of digital warfare to innovative health solutions in the wake of a global health crisis.

The next wave of startups will, undoubtedly, be born out of the confluence of these powerful forces. They will not only have to navigate the waters of a rapidly evolving technological landscape but also attune themselves to the societal heartbeat and the tremors of global events.

The most successful startups will be those that can harness the potential of cutting-edge technology, align with the ethos of their societal context, and turn the challenges posed by global events into opportunities for growth and innovation. It is within this dynamic interplay that the next unicorns will be nurtured, and the startup stories of tomorrow will be written.

Predictions and Advice for Aspiring Entrepreneurs

The Future Landscape of Entrepreneurship

As we stand on the cusp of a new era, entrepreneurship continues to evolve with unprecedented velocity. Advancements in artificial intelligence, the growing accessibility of high-speed internet across the globe, and the normalization of remote work are shaping a future where the barriers to entry for entrepreneurship will continue to diminish.

The digital nomad lifestyle and gig economy are hinting at a world where starting a venture may no longer be confined to the traditional business hubs but dispersed across a global landscape.

Emerging Domains and Technologies

The next wave of startups is likely to be heavily influenced by cutting-edge technologies like quantum computing, biotechnology, and advanced materials science. These fields hold the promise of creating entirely new markets and solving complex problems.

Aspiring entrepreneurs should keep a keen eye on these domains, as the first movers could become the industry leaders of tomorrow.

Sustainable and Social Entrepreneurship

The growing concern for climate change and social inequality is birthing a generation of purpose-driven businesses. The successful entrepreneur of the future is likely to be one who not only understands profit but also the principles of sustainability and social impact.

Companies that can innovate to reduce their environmental footprint while also addressing societal issues will not only stand out but may also benefit from increasingly favorable regulations and consumer goodwill.

Advice for Aspiring Entrepreneurs

For those looking to embark on the entrepreneurial journey, consider the following advice:

- **Embrace Continuous Learning**: The only constant in the world of startups is change. Continuous learning and the ability to adapt are crucial. Stay curious, stay informed, and be prepared to pivot when necessary.

- **Build Resilience**: Entrepreneurship is as much a test of personal endurance as it is of business acumen. Develop a thick skin and learn to view failures as stepping stones to success. Resilience will keep you anchored through the inevitable storms.

- **Foster Meaningful Connections**: In a digital world, never underestimate the power of human connection. Build a strong network, not just for potential business opportunities but for support, mentorship, and collaboration. The value of a community that shares your vision and challenges cannot be overstated.

- **Prioritize Value Over Profit**: Businesses that solve real problems or enhance lives in meaningful ways create value. Focus on creating such value, and profitability will often follow. Remember, the most enduring businesses are those that have found a way to make a difference, not just a profit.

- **Stay Grounded in Ethics**: As technology blurs lines and regulations struggle to keep up, anchor your venture with a strong ethical compass. The trust of your customers and the integrity of your brand are invaluable assets that should be protected at all costs.

In conclusion, as we peer into the future, it's clear that entrepreneurship will continue to be a driving force of innovation and progress. Aspiring entrepreneurs have the opportunity to forge new paths and make their mark on the world.

With passion, perseverance, and a willingness to embrace the unknown, the next generation of entrepreneurs will shape the future one inspired venture at a time.

Conclusion

As our journey through the corridors of creativity and resilience comes to a close, we are left with a mosaic of insights.

"Inspired Ventures: Startups that Began as a Dream" has borne witness to the birth of ideas that stretched the canvas of innovation and entrepreneurship. Each chapter served as a mirror reflecting the tenacity, the ingenuity, and the courage that fuels the startup world.

It's clear that the path of creating a startup is not for the faint-hearted; it is a path of resistance, of towering peaks and crushing valleys.

But within these narratives, we've found a common thread, a relentless passion for building something from nothing and the steadfast belief in one's vision that can weather any storm.

Our voyage has shown us that startups are not just businesses; they are revolutions that start within the entrepreneur's soul. They are crafted not just with keen intellect and sharp skills but with a spirit fired by inspiration.

As we part ways, it's our hope that these stories don't merely end as words on a page, but live on as sparks within you, the reader, the dreamer, the future founder.

May the ventures inspired by dreams continue to shape our world, proving that with imagination, grit, and a dash of daring, anything is possible.

Let this not be an ending, but an invitation, an invitation to dream, to dare, and to do. The world awaits your inspired venture.

Reflecting on The Power of Dreams and Determination

Reflecting on the power of dreams and determination is to recognize the profound impact they have on the journeys of individuals and the history they shape. It is within our most ambitious dreams that the seeds of great ventures are often found.

These dreams, when married with the unwavering determination of their dreamers, have the potential to transcend the boundaries of the ordinary, pushing into realms of extraordinary achievement and innovation.

Dreams are the architects of innovation; they are the silent pulses that energize the weary entrepreneur through countless sleepless nights and the myriad setbacks that are the inevitable companions of any worthwhile endeavor.

Dreams inspire visions of what might be, of potential realities that defy the status quo. They are not bound by the present constraints or past failures but are fueled by the boundless possibilities of what could be achieved with passion and perseverance.

Determination, then, is the engine of this vehicle of change. It's the force that turns the ephemeral into the tangible, the abstract into the concrete.

It is determination that sees a founder through the hundredth pitch to investors, the relentless pursuit of perfection in a product, or the cultivation of a company culture that will withstand the tremors of market shifts and economic downturns.

It is the unwavering commitment to a dream that propels it from the realm of idea into the material world of action and impact.

The stories chronicled in "Inspired Ventures" are testaments to this remarkable synergy between dream and determination. They are tales of ordinary individuals who dared to dream with extraordinary conviction, who chose to see the world not as it was but as it could be.

These entrepreneurs remind us that the bedrock of any significant achievement is often a simple, yet profound, belief in a dream and the tenacity to bring it to life.

They show us that while not all dreams may come to fruition, the act of pursuing them with determination is an invaluable part of the human experience, one that often leads to growth, learning, and sometimes, against all odds, to success that reshapes our world.

As we close the pages of these narratives, we are left with a lingering inspiration and a potent reminder: within each of us lies the potential to dream boldly and the capacity for determination that defies limitations.

Our dreams and our will to achieve them are among the most powerful forces that drive progress, innovation, and transformation, both in the bustling marketplaces of commerce and within the quiet revolutions of our personal lives.

The Lasting Impact of These Startups on Economies, Societies, And Individuals

Startups have an undeniable impact that ripples through economies, societies, and individuals, often bringing about transformative change.

They are the engines of innovation, the crucibles where new ideas are forged into the products, services, and technologies that shape modern life. The growth trajectory of startups often mirrors the evolution of societal needs and the shifting landscapes of global economies.

On an economic level, startups are pivotal in job creation. They contribute significantly to employment, as new businesses require new hands, fresh minds, and diverse skills.

In doing so, they provide opportunities for economic participation across different strata of society, often in new and emerging sectors. Moreover, successful startups can attract substantial investment, both domestic and international, and can lead to the development of entirely new industries.

A single successful startup can elevate a city or even a country's status on the world stage, making it a hub for certain types of innovation, Silicon Valley's rise as the global canter for tech startups is a case in point.

Societally, startups often push the envelope, challenging traditional ways of thinking and doing business. They have the agility to address social issues swiftly, be it through disruptive technology or innovative business models that prioritize sustainability and social impact over profits alone.

For instance, startups have been at the forefront of the sharing economy, changing how people think about ownership and access to resources, leading to more efficient use of assets and potentially less environmental waste.

The cultural influence of startups is also profound. They inspire a culture of entrepreneurship, promoting values such as risk-taking, innovation, and resilience. Startups can become role models, showcasing the virtues of pursuing one's passion and the tangible benefits of hard work and dedication.

This inspiration has a multiplier effect, spurring the creation of more startups and promoting an entrepreneurial mindset even within established organizations.

For individuals, startups often represent the embodiment of the "American Dream" or its equivalent in other nations, the idea that anyone with a good idea and the willingness to work hard can succeed.

Startups democratize opportunity, allowing individuals from diverse backgrounds to carve out their niche. The success stories from these ventures serve as powerful narratives that can empower others to take the leap, potentially leading to a more dynamic and participatory economy.

Furthermore, the products and services that startups introduce can profoundly impact everyday life. From smartphones to sharing economy platforms, from fintech that democratizes access to financial services to health tech startups that personalize medicine, these companies have revolutionized how individuals interact with the world around them.

However, the impact of startups is not always unequivocally positive. The disruptive nature of startups can render existing skills obsolete and industries redundant, leading to economic displacement.

The challenge for societies is to harness the dynamism of startups while mitigating adverse effects through policy, education, and support systems to foster an environment where innovation contributes to the well-being of all.

In the final analysis, the legacy of startups is woven into the fabric of the future. They are not just businesses, but incubators of progress, and their impact will be measured not just in economic metrics, but in the advancement of human society.

Appendix

1: Resources for Aspiring Entrepreneurs

Books

For those embarking on the entrepreneurial journey, knowledge is not just power; it's a necessity. Start with "The Lean Startup" by Eric Ries, which redefined how we approach business creation. This seminal work encourages a lean approach to startup development, emphasizing the importance of agile design and iterative product releases.

Next, "Zero to One" by Peter Thiel offers a counter-intuitive look at innovation and competition, arguing for the pursuit of unique business ideas over incremental improvements.

For insights into the Silicon Valley startup scene, "The Hard Thing About Hard Things" by Ben Horowitz provides an unvarnished look at the challenges of running a startup.

Lastly, for those who need a dose of motivation and personal development, "Mindset: The New Psychology of Success" by Carol S. Dweck, Ph.D., explores the concept of a growth mindset, a crucial trait for any aspiring entrepreneur.

Podcasts

Podcasts offer a portable trove of insights for the entrepreneurial listener. "How I Built This" with Guy Raz dives into the stories behind some of the world's most successful companies, direct from their founders.

"Masters of Scale," hosted by Reid Hoffman, co-founder of LinkedIn, discusses strategies for scaling a business, often featuring high-profile entrepreneurs.

For a daily dose of inspiration, "The Daily Stoic," hosted by Ryan Holiday, applies ancient wisdom to modern entrepreneurial challenges, promoting resilience and clear thinking.

Courses

Education platforms like Coursera, Udemy, and edX have democratized learning, providing courses on every aspect of entrepreneurship.

Whether it's a comprehensive program like Wharton's "Entrepreneurship Specialization" or a more focused course like "The Essential Guide to Entrepreneurship by Guy Kawasaki," these platforms offer knowledge previously confined to the classrooms of top-tier universities.

For those looking for free resources, MIT OpenCourseWare publishes materials from its entrepreneurship courses online at no cost.

Tools

In the digital age, the right tools can provide a significant advantage. Project management software like Asana or Trello helps keep track of tasks and milestones, while financial tools like QuickBooks or FreshBooks simplify accounting.

For market research and competitive analysis, platforms such as CB Insights or CrunchBase provide valuable data.

Social media management tools like Hootsuite or Buffer are crucial for managing an online presence and engaging with customers. Additionally, no entrepreneur should overlook the power of networking; LinkedIn remains an essential platform for connecting with mentors, peers, and potential investors.

The path of entrepreneurship is never walked alone. The wisdom of those who have tread it before, the communities that rally around it, and the tools that facilitate the journey are all part of the ecosystem that supports the entrepreneurial spirit.

By leveraging these resources, aspiring innovators can equip themselves with the knowledge, skills, and mindset needed to transform their vision into reality.

2. Glossary of Startup Terms

1. Angel Investor

An affluent individual who provides capital for a business start-up, usually in exchange for convertible debt or ownership equity.

2. Bootstrapping

Starting a business without external help or capital. Such startups fund development of their company through internal cash flow and are cautious with their expenses.

3. Burn Rate

The rate at which a new company is spending its venture capital to finance overhead before generating positive cash flow from operations; it is a measure of negative cash flow.

4. Crowdfunding

The practice of funding a project or venture by raising monetary contributions from a large number of people, typically via the internet.

5. Disruptive Technology

An innovation that significantly alters the way that consumers, industries, or businesses operate, often displacing old technologies.

6. Elevator Pitch

A brief, persuasive speech that sparks interest in what your startup does. This pitch should be concise enough to be delivered during an elevator ride.

7. Exit Strategy

A planned approach to exiting a situation and is often used to plan the cessation of a business operation or investment.

8. Incubator

An organization designed to accelerate the growth and success of entrepreneurial companies through an array of business support resources and services.

9. Initial Public Offering (IPO)

The first time that the stock of a private company is offered to the public.

10. Lean Startup

A methodology for developing businesses and products that aims to shorten product development cycles and rapidly discover if a proposed business model is viable.

11. Minimum Viable Product (MVP)

A development technique in which a new product or website is developed with sufficient features to satisfy early adopters.

12. Pivot

A structured course correction designed to test a new fundamental hypothesis about the product, strategy, and engine of growth.

13. Runway

The amount of time until a startup goes out of business, assuming income and expenses stay constant.

14. Scale

To grow or expand in a proportional and usually profitable way.

15. Seed Capital

The initial capital used to start a business. Seed capital often comes from the company founders' personal assets or from friends and family.

16. Series A/B/C Funding

Refers to the stage of venture capital financing of a startup company in return for equity. Each "Series" marks the growth phase of the startup, with Series A being an early stage, Series B being a mid-stage, and Series C being a later stage.

17. Startup Ecosystem

The network of individuals (entrepreneurs, venture capitalists, angel investors, mentors), institutions (universities, government agencies, associations), and processes (business competitions, incubators) that interact as a system to create and scale new startup companies.

18. Unicorn

A term in the business world to indicate a privately held startup company valued at over $1 billion.

19. Venture Capital (VC)

Financial capital provided to early-stage, high-potential, high-risk, growth startup companies.

20. Vesting

A legal term that means to give or earn a right to a present or future payment, asset, or benefit.